Don’t Wait for the Period, Leave at the Comma.

Your Rulebook on Disengaging from Negativity and Taking Your Power Back

Janeshia Adams-Ginyard

 Published by: Motivation & Success Publishing (Motivation & Success, LLC).

ISBN Paperback 979-8-9885854-8-0

ISBN Hardcover 979-8-9885854-9-7

Printed in the United States of America.

This book is dedicated to my mother, Gwendolyn Adams-Williams, my maternal grandmother, Virginia Williams (née Cosey), and to my ancestors.

Gwendolyn Adams-Williams, 1951–2002.

Table of Contents

Introduction

Before you start reading this book, I need you to accept one simple premise: You have the power. You've always had the power, and the only reason why you feel powerless is because you gave your power away.

I came to this realization very early in life, after years of watching people allow others to shit on their dreams and their ideas. I've witnessed so many people sit and take it while others openly opposed or demeaned the professional and personal goals they'd set for their lives.

"Why do you want to do that?" "Get a real job." "That's just a dream—you need to be more realistic." "Stop living in a fantasy. You can't do it." "It's too hard!" This is the shit people tell others. They give advice on all of these things that they haven't done themselves—and the person they're giving advice to *actually takes it in*. They listen. They allow this uninformed negativity to go in one ear, stay in the middle of their head, and never leave.

It's simply by listening to these people that you give away your power. You don't have to do that. Where on God's green earth does it say you have to stay and listen to that shit?

That's what I mean when I say you can leave at the comma—you don't have to wait for the period. You don't have to allow people to complete their sentences, their thoughts, their ideas, their opinions on your life. Don't allow them to get to the period. Leave at the comma.

The Comma Is Your Cue

This is not a grammar guide, so I don't want to go too far down the rabbit hole here, but I want to clarify the kind of comma you need to avoid. It's the one that comes after a statement like:

It's too hard to do that, but maybe you should …

That won't work, but this will …

If you don't have enough money, then you should ...

You can't do it that way, so why don't you ...

Based on basic grammar rules, the next part of the sentence will be some kind of clause—not the good kind that might bring kids presents. The kind that imposes itself on your life and decisions and brings negativity into your mental space.

The minute a person with no experience and no quality information starts a sentence this way, and you sense the imminent utterance of something negative, of something contradictory to your set goal or intention—you leave. Do not allow that stuff to sit with you. You are doing yourself a disservice by receiving it. Disengage. Abort the conversation immediately. You don't stay.

I will never understand why people choose to listen to shit that doesn't apply to them. It will never compute in my head the way 1 + 1 = 2 does. This is the state of being that I want you to reach.

That's why I'm writing this book. To remind people: You have the power. You don't have to stay for the period. Leave at the comma. You're doing yourself a disservice if you allow people to speak negativity over your life.

Now, let's discover how you can reclaim and use that power to create the life YOU want! Let's go!

Rule #1:
Be Accountable

When people ask me when I first decided to leave someone at the comma—when I first refused to wait for the period—I tell them I have *never* allowed anyone to complete their sentence. I was in the womb leaving at the commas.

It's how I was raised. It's been instilled in me since birth. But I've watched people throughout my life, whether it be friends in high school, friends in college, acquaintances, or colleagues, and I've listened to their stories. Every time someone presents me with a new story about how they let someone with no experience and no knowledge speak negativity over them, I always wonder why they would do that. Would they allow someone who doesn't own a house to tell them not to buy a house?

I've never been someone to do that. My mom instilled very good morals in me. She made sure my twin sister, Jamea, and I were well-rounded, so not only were we excellent students, but we were great athletes, awesome musicians, public speakers, and fluent in sign language.

I was always taught to know that I have the power to dictate where I want to go in life. If I have faith, I can get anywhere I want. All I have to do is believe.

Growing up, vision boards were a very big tool in my household. I learned early that I could speak something into existence—walk as if it's already happened—and it's going to happen. I absorbed lessons like "success is inevitable" and "no is not an option." In the womb, I was destined for greatness. And I'm not the only one—you were too! You are destined for greatness.

Somewhere along the line, you allowed someone to take you off track and disrupt your path to greatness. Well, I'm reminding you to get your ass back on the road, OK? You made a U-turn, took a detour, and now you're lost. Let me help find and lead you back to the path you should be on.

Six-year-old Janeshia on school picture day.

Jamea and Janeshia after returning from Washington for 1998 USATF Junior Olympics. Janeshia placed in many events, including the heptathlon where she placed third and had several personal bests.

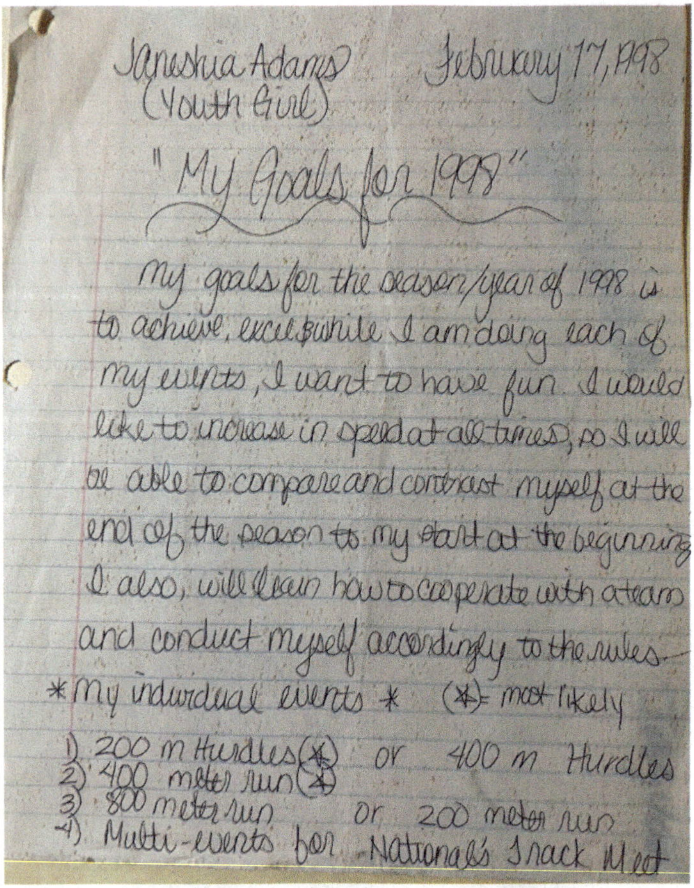

Janeshia Adams (Youth Girl) February 17, 1998

"My Goals for 1998"

My goals for the season/year of 1998 is to achieve, excel & while I am doing each of my events, I want to have fun. I would like to increase in speed at all times, so I will be able to compare and contrast myself at the end of the season to my start at the beginning I also, will learn how to cooperate with a team and conduct myself accordingly to the rules.

*My individual events * (✱)= most likely

1) 200 m Hurdles (✱) or 400 m Hurdles
2) 400 meter run (✱)
3) 800 meter run or 200 meter run
4) Multi-events for National's Track Meet

A report in which Janeshia was asked by her club track coach, Robert King, to write down her goals for the 1998 track season. The letter reads:

My goals for the season/year of 1998 is to achieve, excel & while I am doing each of my events, I want to have fun. I would like to increase in speed at all times, so I will be able to compare and contrast myself at the end of the season to my start at the beginning. I also, will learn how to cooperate with a team and conduct myself accordingly to the rules.

** My individual events * (☆)=most likely*

1) *200 m Hurdles(☆)* *or* *400 m Hurdles*
2) *400 meter run(☆)*
3) *800 meter run* *or* *200 meter run*
4) *Multi-events for National's Track Meet*

Taking Back Power

Sometimes, to regain something, you simply have to stop giving it away. That is the case with power. To reclaim it, you need to stop giving power over your life and mindset to people who don't deserve it. If you have to ask for permission, you're not in control. If you're seeking approval, then you've stayed to see what's after the comma.

Most people get thrown off their path by people who are not in control. They are not the decision-makers. I laugh sometimes just thinking about it. If you are asking for permission, you are not in control.

You can't tell me what I can't do. I can do whatever I want. It's very simple. I remember watching my mom one time ask to speak to a manager at a store. The associate helping her said, "They're just going to tell you the same thing I told you." My mom said, "No. You have to go get your manager, which means you don't have that power. And you cannot speak for someone else. That's their brain. You have no authority." Again, people who have to ask for permission are not in control.

Janeshia's mother, Gwendolyn, at IHOP during an annual family trip to Las Vegas.

Redefine Who Matters

We make life way too complicated. I'm here to tell you it's not that goddamned hard. Don't be so busy trying to please people who don't matter, people who are not going to be around at the end when you're crossing the finish line in first place. They won't even be there. And you're worried about how you look to them, how you sound, if they're going to be offended. Stop dimming your light because people can't handle your luminosity. That's one of my mottos. I will never dim my light. At all. I have never had to redefine who matters in my life, because, for me, I have always been the one who matters.

When I was about ten, I was walking around the high school track with my mom, and I saw a girl running while her mom timed her. Wondering what she was doing, I went over and asked her what she was running for. She told me she was on a track team, and I got the information for the club, then went out to that track club and joined it with my twin sister. Just like that, track immediately became a part of our childhood.

When you are the one who matters to you, you start figuring out what you gravitate toward. Track was one of those things, and within two years, at twelve years old, I was a national champion. Eventually, I realized I could use track as a way to get a scholarship to make sure my mom didn't have to pay for my postsecondary education. Sure enough, I ran track in college.

Janeshia's third grade school photo.

Growth through Accountability

If you do not hold yourself accountable, if you cannot be honest with your actions and the results they give, then there's no room for growth, which means no room for elevation and progress.

Everything comes down to decision-making because decision-making is what leads you to go right or left, good or bad. I've learned that accountability is a result of the decisions that you make, whether good or bad. I navigate this planet with a mindset to be smart in my decision-making so that I have fewer negative consequences or bad results. I have no desire to suffer a negative consequence, so I always make sure that I'm accountable for my actions. That is how I grow.

Accountability is just another way of being honest with yourself. Life is much easier if you're able to be accountable with yourself because that means you're able to be accountable with others. You won't be afraid to own up to mistakes and apologize immediately. You won't be excuse driven, you'll be solutions driven.

There are always those who try to find an excuse for something. "Oh my God, my circumstance, my environment." Yet, some people grew up in households full of crack, cocaine, drugs, and alcoholism, people who were beaten or abused, and they have turned out great. Then you have other people who have had silver spoons, trust funds, and maids, and they ain't done shit! There is no science to it. It just comes down to decision-making and accountability.

Busting through Accountability Barriers

I think what hinders people from being accountable to themselves is the vulnerability that comes with it. A lot of people don't want to be honest, which is part of my accountability definition. Not being honest means you're not being vulnerable. It means you are not willing to say you fucked up, you made a bad decision, you went left and you should've gone right. It's not hard to be accountable. You must get past the fear of acknowledging your mistakes and apologizing for them.

If you're honest with yourself, it's so much easier to be honest with somebody else. It goes back to the saying, "How can you love somebody else if you don't love yourself?"

It's the same shit. If you're accountable to yourself, it is so much easier to be accountable to somebody else.

I think another challenge for people to be accountable is the fear of future disappointment or being let down. You have to get over the let-down factor and instead look at everything as a learning experience, as an opportunity for growth. Life is nothing but learning experiences and growth if you allow it to be.

Change your mindset when you're accountable with yourself. Don't assume it means you're bad or worthless; just acknowledge that you're simply being honest about the decision you made. Once you realize that shit doesn't work, change it. That decision did not produce positive results, so do not do it again.

You have the freedom to change. That's the beauty of being an autonomous being. For some strange reason, people forget that. You have the power to just change. To alter that shit and pivot. Real quick. It's like when you step on someone's foot and say, "Yo, my bad, I'm sorry." Well, say that to yourself. "Damn, self, I'm sorry. I fucked up."

Be honest with your decision-making and your choices, and then navigate accordingly. If you mess up, change and do what's right. Don't stay in the funk or the wrong, because that's when excuses and self-deprecation show up.

When I ran track in high school, I was a record-setting hurdler and a heptathlete. I was a little Jackie Joyner-Kersee. One time, I was running in a preliminary hurdle event to qualify for the California Interscholastic Federation (CIF) finals, and I'd gotten into the habit of second-guessing hurdle six after coming off hurdle five. But second-guessing made me stutter, so my race wasn't smooth and I lost time. In a race with only eight hurdles, time is of the essence. One small stutter can be the determining factor of whether I will advance to the next round.

I had to make up the lost time from hurdle seven to get to hurdle eight and haul ass to cross the finish line so I could make it to the finals scheduled for the following week.

My mom and my coach were like, "Janeshia, why do you stutter at the top of the curve? You jeopardized making it to the finals because you did all that stuttering. You've trained this whole season for this. If you don't make it to the finals, you won't make state. That's the goal here. Everything you need, you've got. The training, the skills—all of it. You've been doing this for years."

They were absolutely right. And I immediately admitted it with no excuses. No one made me stutter. No one made me second-guess my ability to run a smooth race. That was me, in my head, doing some funky shit, and it almost jeopardized my entire season.

Let me tell you—at that next race, which was finals, accountability came in full force. *You cannot stutter*, I told myself. *Janeshia, you got this. You will not stutter. Trust your stride. If anything, run faster. Don't fucking slow up. Why would you go from running in perfect stride to choppy, choppy, choppy, choppy, choppy? It doesn't make sense. What the fuck are you doing?*

During finals, I did not stutter. I kept my same stride, went faster, had a smooth race, and I fucking won CIF. I was the CIF champion in the 300m hurdles!

I had to be accountable for the stutter. I had to acknowledge that it almost cost me my season. I had to sit down with myself and say, *You cannot do that shit again. If your goal is to go to the finals for the State of California, that shit you just pulled is not going to fly, because next week, everybody's going to be fucking* hungry. *They're going to be just as hungry as you for first place, and if you don't get your shit together, you are not going to be on the podium.*

Between the week of my stutter and finals, I worked more on going over the hurdle with the wrong leg than with the right leg. Why? Because I said, *If I get to that hurdle on the wrong leg, I'm still jumping it*. So I prepared myself to jump, no matter which leg was the lead leg.

You, too, need to be so on point that you can opposite-leg that shit. You just aren't going to stop. Just go. Your life will be better if you go and fuck up, do the wrong leg, do the wrong arm, whatever, rather than stop completely, disrupt the momentum, and damper the motivation.

Finally, you have to know other people see your greatness—just like my mom and my coach saw mine. Your haters already see your greatness. They see your greatness before you do.

I stuttered at hurdle six. What's your hurdle six? What are you allowing to make you stutter—even though you know you've got this shit? Remind yourself that you're destined for greatness. Everything you need to get over your hurdle six, you have. Just fucking run. Don't stop. Be the Kool-Aid Man running through that brick wall. Just fucking go.

A San Gabriel Valley League track meet in 2001. Janeshia placed first in the 100m hurdles.

Masters Meet at Cerritos College in 2001. Janeshia would qualify for the CIF-State Track and Field Championships in the 300m hurdles.

Janeshia running the second leg of the Gahr High School 4x400m relay at the Mt. Sac Relays.

Setting Effective Goals for Accountability

My number one piece of accountability advice for people is to *accomplish the mission*, whatever the mission might be, even if it's going to the grocery store to purchase everything from the grocery list. How many times have you been to the grocery store or Target and gotten distracted and left without what you went there for in the first place? You left the store with everything that you didn't even go there to get, but the one thing you needed, you never even made it to that aisle.

Assess your mission in its entirety, from top to bottom, and start to fulfill the fundamental requirements. Let's say you want to be an actor. Assess what you're doing toward that goal. Do you have good headshots? Have you taken acting classes? Have you done theater? Have you done improv? Have you googled "What is acting"? What do you need to become an actor?

My mom always said, "Be a student of the sport," whatever that sport is. Accounting, athletics, optometry, education—it doesn't matter. The "sport" is the thing you're going after. When I made my transition from acting to stunt work, I took my mom's words and became a student of the sport. I did my homework on stunts. What do stunt people do? How do they perform? What kind of equipment do they use? Who are the top stunt coordinators?

After my research, I hired a private gymnastics coach and picked up basic tumbling, because I saw a lot of stunt people doing flips and aerial work. I needed to have some air awareness because I didn't know how to do anything outside of a cartwheel and a round-off. I needed to learn how to do a back handspring and how to work on a trampoline.

People tell me all the time they want to get into acting. I always ask them, "What are you doing toward that goal?" Just saying what you want to do isn't shit. What are you doing? How are you holding yourself accountable to get where you want to be? Every actor I know has taken some type of classes or had private coaching. They've got quality, industry-standard headshots done by a studio or industry professional. They are students of the sport.

Janeshia with twin sister Jamea, eating a clam chowder bread bowl in San Francisco at Fisherman's Wharf.

Janeshia working as an on-air radio personality at 106KMEL in San Francisco.

A high school graduation photo of Janeshia and Jamea. Janeshia graduated with high honors.

Holding Others Accountable

Take responsibility for your actions, but don't forget to hold others accountable too. Many people believe holding others accountable for their actions and choices is a problem, but it's time to change that perception. If you're one of those people, then the first thing you have to eliminate from your mind is the word *problem*. That is negative. Accountability is not conflict, it is resolution. People who can't communicate always think everything is a problem, and it's not. If you can articulate and use your words, you're already halfway there.

Frame your mind to understand that you're reaching for a solution and it's not a conflict. If the person you're talking to views it as a conflict, that might be a red flag for you to pay attention to, because communication is not conflict.

Remember, communication is dialogue. Never be afraid to speak up. You should always be able to say, "Hey, I don't like how you treated me. I don't like what you said to me. That wasn't nice, what you did. That was not right."

If someone thinks that's conflict, fuck them. That's not conflict. That's you effectively communicating your autonomous power. It's you telling them how to talk to you, how to treat you. Telling them how to communicate with you so they can get the best from you. Eliminate from your mind that asking for accountability from others is conflict because it's about the solution.

Imagine you're in a relationship. Ask your partner, "Do you want this to work? If you want it to work, let's communicate, let's have a dialogue, let's have a conversation on how I expect this from you, so when I come to you, I'm expecting you to do X, Y, or Z." It's just conversation.

When you avoid conversation and hold stuff in, it's unhealthy. You are a ticking time bomb that will eventually detonate. Let's not do that. Not everything is conflict. Conversation and accountability are solution-driven because you're finding the solution on how to be honest with yourself so that you can be honest with others. It's very simple: just talk it out.

With that, make sure the tone you use when talking is appropriate. You want people to hear what is being said, so tone comes into play. Watch how you say what you have to share.

Accepting Your Level of Accountability

When you begin to hold yourself accountable and bring that accountability into your relationship with others, you have to be comfortable being different—because not everyone will be on the same level as you.

I accept that I'm different. I accept that I was raised with amazing tools and morals my mother instilled in me. I accept that I operate at a higher frequency than most. With that being said, I try not to let it frustrate me, knowing that the majority of the people I might come across are not at that level.

This means I have to acknowledge what they're good at. I have to acknowledge the other things they bring to the table, because even knowing that I'm at a higher frequency, I don't know it all.

We're all pawns at the end of the day. God has put people in my life as pawns, and He's put me in the lives of others as a pawn—this is how we all learn from one another and bless one another's lives. Everyone brings something to the table. Teamwork makes the dream work, and I wouldn't be this high-functioning person if I didn't have all the people around me supplying whatever it is they're giving.

Jen Du Plessis said it great: "Not everybody has the same currency, so figure out the currency that people operate and give you."

It does wonders when you can tell people in your circle to hold you accountable, when you can say to them, "Hey, look, if I mess up, tell me, let me know. Don't feel like I'll chew your head off."

It takes a village and a tribe. There's a reason why LeBron James is LeBron James. His mom, his family, and the people around him supported him and held him accountable, but besides them, he held himself accountable. Make sure you have people around who don't tell you what you want to hear, but who tell you what you *need* to hear to be better.

I think that's how we make ourselves better.

I loved Michael Jackson to death. He's still one of my favorite musicians, but goddamnit, he surrounded himself with yes-men. I don't want those people in my life. I don't want people sticking me with fucking Propofol because I'm saying, "Stick me with Propofol." No. Tell me, "That shit ain't good for you. Let's do something else."

Rule #2:
Show Gratitude

At the end of Chapter 1, I talked about how it takes a village and how teamwork makes the dream work. If you want to continue to benefit from the team effort creating your life, then you need to show gratitude.

When you have gratitude, you recognize that you know you didn't achieve everything by yourself. You are grateful and you are thankful because you could not do this life alone.

Success is not a status attained overnight. It came with the help of other people, and we should all be thankful. But my gratitude will always go first to God. I am grateful for the breath of life. If I wasn't alive, I would not be able to move. If the people who are in my life weren't alive, then He wouldn't be able to use them as pawns to get the best out of me.

Gratitude is essential. I cannot start my day without being thankful to God, for Him and His Son Jesus, because He is the most grateful person. He gave His Son for us.

I navigate the planet knowing that gratitude is like love. God loves me, I love Him, and I'm so incredibly grateful.

Ultimately, gratitude is an acknowledgment that I know I did not do this on my own. God has placed people in my life to help me get where I am. When you have gratitude, you're showing thanks and appreciation to the creator. You tap into the higher source and acknowledge that this is bigger than you. You're calling out the people who have helped you get to where you need to go.

Every time someone comes to my booth at comic conventions, whether they buy anything, I say, "Thank you so much for stopping by my booth and saying hi. Thank you for chatting with me. Thank you for even wanting to see me and speak with me. Thank you for that." I tell my team, "Thank you. Thank you for putting up with me. Thank you for your help."

You can build success on discipline. But if you want to be a better person, start being grateful. Start being thankful. You will feel so much love and relief, like a weight being lifted off your shoulders, when you can be grateful. This has to be done so often that it does not become practice but becomes your lifestyle.

We have to be in a place where not only are we grateful that we receive, but we are grateful to give. When you can give and not expect anything in return, that is a rewarding place to be. All you have to do is find a moment in the middle of the chaos that is life to stop and think, "Wow, I'm so thankful for this breath of life. Thank you. Thank you, God, for waking me up this morning. I'm thankful that I'm here and that my family is not preparing a funeral. Thank you for the movement of my limbs and eyes to see."

It's not hard.

Prayer is an essential part of Janeshia's life.

Taking Half a Beat

I operate from a place of abundance. When you're operating from a place of abundance, gratitude is the natural side effect. And if you don't feel it immediately, just wait—give it space to come in.

I play in a stunt softball league and normally when I catch the ball, I immediately throw it, as soon as the ball hits my glove. That can make the trajectory wonky, so the ball doesn't always go to my target, because I just caught the ball and boom, I threw it. My coach, who calls me Hollywood, will say, "Half a beat, Hollywood. Take half a beat."

So I tell people, "Take half a beat and let that gratitude come in. Let that gratitude enter your space, that thankful space. You have it, but you're all over the place and you're choosing not to take the half beat to acknowledge."

Half a beat is all it takes to allow gratitude to cut through the chaos of life and feel it positively affect you. Just taking that half a beat and having that gratitude and that grateful energy in your life says a lot. You will notice your life change. If you need to, start a gratitude journal or have a sign with the word *grateful* in your kitchen, or use the word *grateful* as a screensaver on your phone. Whatever it is, gratitude needs to be acknowledged daily because that's when you will see your life improve.

For Those Struggling with Gratitude

If you are struggling with gratitude, I have a challenge for you. This is a practice my mom had me and my twin sister do whenever we didn't do what we were supposed to. It's a thing called *standards*.

Here's how I would describe it: Have you ever seen *The Simpsons* intro? In it, there's a part where Bart Simpson writes on the chalkboard the same thing over and over and over. In the original intro, he wrote, "I will not skateboard in the halls." That practice is called standards, or writing lines. If my sister or I didn't do something, like finish homework we were supposed to do, my mom would say, "You guys, one hundred standards." Then we would have to write, "I will have my homework finished on time" one hundred times. Trust me—after doing a couple hundred standards, you'll work to not make the same mistake twice. Accountability comes into play real quick.

Essentially, standards are a way of training yourself. You can also say your phrase out loud. Then you hear yourself and hold yourself accountable.

My challenge to you is to write "I am grateful" fifty times per day. I am training you to be grateful. You can start today's standards on the next page. Do this daily and consistently, and it won't take long before you've formed a habit of gratefulness.

Ready to get started? Write your standards on the lines provided.

I am grateful.

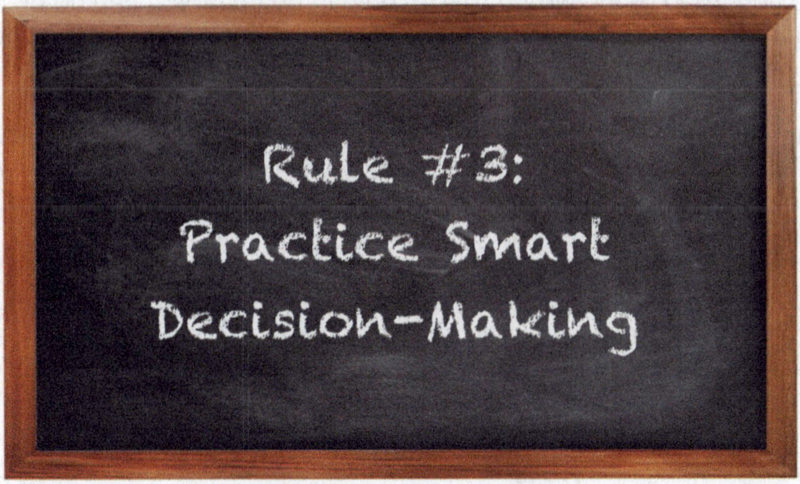
Rule #3:
Practice Smart
Decision-Making

When you stay after the comma and listen to what someone says all the way to the period, you aren't just making a choice—you're making a decision. You know what else is a decision? Leaving at the comma and NOT staying for the period.

The point is, everything you do in life is the result of a decision you make. Your decision-making leads to consequences, whether good or bad. I'm always focused on making decisions that will lead me toward consequences that are prosperous, fulfilling, and abundant.

Excuses or Decisions

Decision-making is vital to one's life because it can send you down the right road or the wrong road. You can go up or you can go down. You can progress or you can digress, all based on a very simple decision.

Few people will admit that their negative consequences stem from poor decisions, however. Instead, they will find an excuse. They will come up with reasons why they *can't* do something, instead of coming up with reasons why they *can*.

I can do what I do because I came from a strong, Black, single mother. I operate and navigate this planet strong and confident because of my single African American mother, who had a great job as a senior accountant at Xerox. But we can all learn from the people—or person—who raised us. We can take good lessons even from bad things they might have done, so I don't want to hear your sob story about your single mother. I'm the way I am because of my single mother. I am grateful because of what she instilled in me. The tools and morals I received, the church services I attended, the faith she gave us, the confidence to ask questions, and the encouragement to engage in conversations with people from different walks of life.

I know how to play the piano. I was offered a music scholarship. I ran track. I was offered track scholarships. I'm great at math—all because of my mother. Even if your single mother didn't put in the same effort, you can learn from what she *didn't* do. There are plenty of stories about people who were raised by single parents in terrible situations, yet they still grow up making good decisions and holding themselves accountable. Hell, I know people who grew up with both parents and aren't even a small percentage of the way I am. Having both parents is no guarantee you'll be an upstanding, productive human being, so we can't use that as an excuse. We just can't.

My point is, we have to get out of the habit of making excuses. Decide whatever card you're dealt, whatever hand you're given, how do you fuckin' play it? That is your choice. You decide how to play your hand.

If you had issues growing up—maybe you felt less than or insecure—there are ways to get help with that. Choose to find out how you can become a better person. I had to figure out what I needed to do to become the amazing Emmy-nominated stunt woman that I am because no one in my family did stunts. Hell, I didn't even know what stunts were. I came from a senior accountant and a musician.

Stop making excuses and start making choices that will lead you to abundance and prosperity.

Making Better Decisions

One of the most important ways to improve your decision-making is to remember that you have the power and you don't have to settle.

I often see people settle for less than they deserve. No one has to do that. People are quick to say yes to some shit that won't be beneficial for them in the long run. But there's power in saying no.

People ask me all the time for advice to get into the movie industry, and the number one thing I tell them is that there's power in saying no.

You don't always have to say yes. That yes might not be beneficial for you. "You do not have to give in to the pressure or bullying on these production sets. That yes might sacrifice your morals," I tell them. You don't have to do the casting couch. You can trust your skills, work harder, and know that the right gig, the right role, the right job will come to you through your hard work and trusting your skills.

Every day we're given a choice—the choice to do right or wrong. Learning to say no is a tremendous tool for making the right choices.

Let's say some person is asking a married man, "Hey, you want to hang out with these chicks?"

All he has to say to stay on the right path is no. "Nah, man, that's not for me. I'm good. I got a wife." He needs to be accountable, to be honest, to be truthful.

For those trying to get ahead in their field, when a person asks, "Hey, do you want to go out and do some unsavory type of work?"

Instead of sacrificing their values to try to get ahead, they can say, "Nah, I'm OK. I'll just go to my job. I'll work hard. I'll apply for new jobs."

Before you make any decisions, you've got to think of the consequences. Will this choice be good or bad for my life? What happens if I get caught? Where will this leave me? Will doing this set me back or move me forward, legally? Will my mental health be affected?

You're free. You have the power. It seems so simple, but people forget they control their own lives. Don't give your power away. Don't allow anyone to steal your dreams. Dreams are free—they didn't cost you a dime, so why would you give them away?

Avoiding the Instant Gratification Trap

Success is not a status gained overnight. It is a long game.

You are an autonomous being and you don't have to travel the road that won't produce any good. Too often, people gravitate toward instant gratification versus playing the long game. To succeed, you need to change that focus from short-term relief and focus on your endurance.

When you decide to make choices that are better for your life—those that confirm your power over your life—some people are going to be upset and angry that you have decided not to give them the power anymore. You must be OK with that.

For so long, people have gotten used to you giving your power away. They've grown accustomed to you being weak and settling. When you start saying, "No more, it's done. I disengage from you," it will be an issue, but you have to know that it is not *your* issue.

When your decision-making starts putting you first, it's saying, "I don't have to wait for the period, I can leave at the comma. What you're saying doesn't apply to me. It's not helping me grow. I'm trying to reach my destination, my goal, while you're trying to send me along this detour. No more. I disengage."

When your decision-making begins to work in your favor, it will upset some people. But be OK with that because that is not your issue.

Rule #4:
Channel Your Inner
Leader

Essentially, when you decide to improve your decision-making skills, leave at the comma, embrace accountability, and show gratitude, you will become the leader of your life. But what does it really mean to be a leader?

Defining a Leader

When I started taking on speaking engagements in 2017, one particular attendee told me, "You make me feel like I can take on Mike Tyson." To me, that is the epitome of being a leader—giving others a feeling of confidence they've never had before.

Everybody wants to feel like they can take on the champ, but a leader shows them that they can. A leader inspires, encourages, and motivates so strongly that even the weakest person feels some degree of change. Their mindset shifts. Negative thoughts will be replaced with thoughts like, "I can do," "I can be," and "I will."

I am a leader and, as such, people see and believe everything that comes out of my mouth. Great leadership is observed through the actions of the leader—not through the words they say.

It has been said, "Always witness for Christ, and when necessary, use words." I want to make sure that people can see the love for Christ in me without me saying, "I believe in Jesus! Team Jesus!" Through my actions, people can see His light shine through me and that I am a believer. They can see I possess great love and gratitude without me saying, "I have love and gratitude within. I'm a child of the King."

Just as I walk in the light of my love for Jesus, I walk the life of a forthright, honest, accountable leader without having to tell everyone that's what I am.

A great leader is someone people want to follow without the person saying, "Follow me. Do what I'm doing." Great leaders lead by example. They are transparent and reliable. They can communicate effectively and spark a fire under someone's ass that makes them want to do and be better.

Parents as Leaders

My mom is a quintessential example of a great leader. I remember sitting in front of the TV every Saturday and Sunday when I was seven years old, watching football and basketball with my brother. During the games, I would provide commentary. I could recite to you every player's stats—what they did and where they came from—at seven years old. As a child, I'd watch sportscasters like Pam Oliver and Bob Costas, knowing that I wanted to be a sports commentator and sign language interpreter for deaf athletes, but also knowing that sports would get me to college. My mom sat with me and often said, "You can be a sports commentator just like Pam Oliver."

Parents must be involved in cultivating their kids' interests. While running track certainly influenced my life, my mom telling me I could reach my intended goal was the leadership I needed to help push me in the right direction.

As great leaders, parents also need to prepare their kids for a variety of outcomes. My mom prepared me for everything that I've gotten up until now. She made sure I was well-rounded. I was entered into oratorical contests and had the tools to be a public speaker. I was extremely proficient in math, was a very good student athlete, and could play three instruments. Every day after track practice, we went home and ran in place for an additional thirty minutes. After already being exhausted from a full practice, I had more work to do at home. Working on my form and breathing. She had me putting in the extra work to be better, to be great.

I was a multi-hyphenate before I even knew the word *multi-hyphenate* existed! I think where many parents fail is by trying to make their kids home in one thing or nothing at all.

It's your job as a parent to find the means for your child to do whatever they are interested in because your child never asked to be here. My twin sister and I didn't ask to be in this world, so my mom made sure we would be functioning, skilled human beings.

When you're well-rounded, you develop skills from all those areas that can, in turn, be applied in your life as you progress and age. You gain so much knowledge that can always be applied along your journey. Those skills will allow you to converse and connect with people—and who knows how many doors that will open.

My involvement with sports and youth athletics opened many doors. I didn't just run track. I also played volleyball in high school. As an adult, I had the opportunity to do sports modeling for different Nike campaigns, and I became a brakeman on the US National Bobsled Team. Thanks to my mom and her parental discipline, I was prepared for every opportunity that came my way.

With discipline comes accountability, and she made us accountable for our actions so that we would want to do better and be upstanding citizens in this world.

I don't think parents tell their kids enough that they can be whatever they want to be. One of my goals with this book is to make sure you never listen to people who tell you what you can't do—and there are a lot of them out there. A good leader—and parents, as leaders—should focus on what their child CAN do. I think many parents just drop the ball by not giving kids the encouragement they need. They don't speak positively; they speak with semantic limitations. I tell people all the time, "The sky is not the limit because the sky is way too low."

Don't dim your kids' light. They're showing you what they want to do—even through things you might consider misbehavior. If they're talking all the time and not listening, maybe put them in some oratorical contests. Maybe there is some interest in being a public speaker, news reporter, or even boxing ring announcer. Who knows? Whatever it is, help them figure it out. Home in on the positive skills and don't tell them what they can't do.

US Bobsled duo, Jamia Jackson (driver, front) and Janeshia (brakeman, back) at the start of Run 2 of the North American Cup in Calgary, Alberta, Canada, on November 15, 2006. The duo placed sixth on the podium.

Janeshia on race day at the North American Cup in Calgary, Alberta, Canada, on November 15, 2006. North American Cup is a part of the International Bobsleigh & Skeleton Federation.

Janeshia in her CAL track uniform. Go Bears!

Ignoring the Hate

Great leaders are always going to have haters. Not everyone will follow you. Yet often, the people who don't follow you still respect you. I know some people probably can't stand me because I'm so high frequency, but they respect me, and that's the sign of a great leader.

I know I have an energy and a frequency that is high. Some people want to touch and be near that because they know it's going to help elevate them. This energy is going to motivate, inspire, and light a fire under their ass. But my haters receive that same frequency. That fire is lighting up their asses too, even if they are rebellious or jealous. They are there, but I don't pay attention to them.

Haters, on the other hand, pay attention to you every day. Even your followers don't pay attention to you every day, but your haters do—and that is proof of their respect. These haters will retweet your quotes without giving you credit and they are going to share your philosophies without mentioning where they came from. And in that sense, you as a leader are doing your job regardless of the haters. You are ensuring that your message is heard by everybody.

I don't discriminate in my message. As a leader, I tell everybody what to do, how to act, how to inspire, how to encourage, how to be better. And my haters help me spread that message.

Now, if someone doesn't want to receive that message, that is not my responsibility. I am operating from a place of abundance by sharing this information, these nuggets and jewels. The acceptance of the message is on them.

Ultimately, the signal the haters send from their frequency is so much lower than mine, their energy doesn't transfer to me. It's like static on a radio. Their vibe is not coming through. Their message can not be deciphered.

Choosing Right

A great leader, one who operates out of abundance, will always experience increased overflow and prosperity. But remember, you are only a great leader when you always do right.

I could be standing on Mount Rushmore all by myself, and I would still only choose to do good, to do the right thing. My mom raised me that way. She always said, "You always do right. There is nowhere on this planet where you choose to do wrong. You do right, and if that means you're standing by yourself, you be OK with that. Because you're not by yourself. God is right there with you, and He's got your back."

I've been in plenty of situations where I've had to stand alone because I chose to do right. I chose to speak up. I am known in the industry for speaking up when someone is talking crazy, being disrespectful, when a person is talking down to or belittling the extras and background performers. There are a number of actors who could tell you, "I think Janeshia got in trouble because she stood up for us," or, "I think Janeshia got in trouble because she told them that they were talking disrespectfully to the background." I'm OK with that. That's how I was raised.

I will “take a beating” if it means I’m standing up for what’s right and doing good because I know I’ll be rewarded in the long run. My decision to do right weighs far more than me going along with the masses doing wrong.

Leaders must make difficult decisions every single day. You have to know that as a leader, you can’t please everybody. There is no way to walk this planet and please everybody. It just ain’t gonna happen. Hell, Jesus came to save the world, and He got the worst beating on planet Earth. I know I will not please everyone, but that does not mean I don’t navigate with the intention of doing what’s right.

As a leader, doing what’s right is not always the norm. As crazy as it sounds, doing what’s right is not always accepted. But for me, I will not live according to those standards. I will always resort to being fair and honest, reliable, accountable, and transparent.

Don’t be afraid to be on the mountain by yourself when you have made the decision to do right. Your good will pay off. You will be rewarded. People think it’s more fun to lie or do wrong, but that’s a lie within itself! Because those consequences are going to come back. What you do in the dark will come to light.

It’s OK to Follow

Leaders carry a weight on their shoulders because they’re representing a lot of people and standing up against those doing wrong. It’s not for everyone—and you don’t have to ask to become a leader. You either are one or you are not.

No one told me I was going to be a leader. It is simply inside me. No one will tell you you’re going to be a leader. It’s either in you or it’s not. We’ve all made decisions and found our place. No one had to tell Michael Jordan he was going to be a leader.

If you aren’t a leader, then you could be a follower, and that, too, comes with standards and responsibilities. If you are a follower, then be a great follower. Be the best follower. In all things, teamwork makes the dream work. A great coach without players isn’t going to win the game.

I, Janeshia, am the coach and the leader for a lot of people, but damn it, my players are amazing. They see my commitment, actions, and work ethic. They believe in me, which makes them believe in the team and where we are headed. This team is a fast-moving locomotive that's going to increase prosperity and abundance.

You may not choose to be a leader or a follower, but as a follower, you DO choose your leader. Choose one who brings out powerful, positive qualities in you. Keep people in your circle, entourage, or clique who provide encouraging words and messages. Otherwise, you're doing yourself a disservice.

Rule #5:
Know That You Have
The Power

Ignoring your personal power is one of the biggest mistakes you can make. If you don't realize you have personal power, then you don't know what you're giving away—or what you can get back.

Personal power is a deeply instilled knowledge that you have the influence to create and change any behavior and knowing that you are the final decision-maker in your life.

We all have personal power, but not everybody uses their power. Many have given their power away, whether they know it or not. They allow others to make choices and decisions about what they have going on in their life, uncontested. Key decisions are made, whether in conversation or action, that go unchallenged because folks have relinquished their power into the hands of others.

What do I mean? This happens when you allow others to make decisions about what you have going on in your life. For example, you tell a friend that you have a great new business idea that can change the world. Your friend responds with, "Why would anyone want that?" or, "You can't do that." Or, "That is going to cost way too much." Because of what they said, you decide to not move forward and make your idea a reality.

You, my friend, just gave away your power.

When you allow others to choose your path, dictate your life's direction, or set the parameters for what is possible for you to achieve, you give away your power.

The Problem with Relinquishing Power

When you give away your power, you're giving your decision-making abilities to somebody else and allowing them to influence your behavior based on their own set of rules and biases. If, instead, you keep your decision-making power, the only person who can influence your behavior is you.

I think people overcomplicate life far too often, usually out of fear. When you do that, at some point along the way, you'll end up giving away some of your power. We all know when we're trying to flex or show off or trying to keep up with the Joneses. We know what's in our bank account and what our debt looks like, and we know whether we can truly afford three houses, a Rolls-Royce, and a Rolex. But somewhere along the way, people become scared to be their authentic selves, so they try to disguise who they are and walk around living a lie.

That is what I mean by relinquishing your power. If you know you don't have the savings or income to support some crazy expense, but you buy it anyway so you look like you can afford it, you are giving up your power.

Let me say it again: When you allow society and outside influences to drive your decisions so that they no longer align with what you've got going on in your life, you have given away your power.

Some people try to excuse doing this, covering it up with excuses. The truth is, there is no excuse. Putting on a show that isn't an honest reflection of who you are and what you can afford is just you being weak and scared, and that is a decision you've made. Essentially, you have decided that you're not going to live as your authentic self.

Don't think you're the only person in society with pressure. There are eight billion people in this world—and every single one of them faces pressure. When you answer that pressure by relinquishing your power, you're choosing to live this way.

I choose to live authentically and honestly as Janeshia, and I don't care what anybody thinks. If I want something I can't afford, guess what? I'm not going to get it just because someone else did. That is my decision-making that aligns with my life and my finances. I'm not going to go into debt to acquire it, I'm not going to steal it, and I'm not going to lie or cheat to get it.

Overcoming Fear of No

Fear is a weakness. The first thing you can do to get over it is to start saying no. Part of what's keeping you weak and afraid is your tendency to keep saying yes to actions and commitments that don't align with you. Start saying no. Be honest with yourself and stop thinking your no is going to be offensive.

Also, remember that no is a complete sentence. It amazes me when people want to give an excuse or disclaimer for saying no. You don't give an excuse or disclaimer for your yes, so why do you need to do so for your no?

I said that to somebody. They wanted me to explain my no. I told them no—I'm not explaining my no. You don't have me explain my yes, and that is an answer too. Yes or no. Period. Stop giving people disclaimers for your decisions. No is no. You don't owe anyone anything else.

People navigate this earth thinking they owe people long explanations and disclaimers. As harsh as it might sound, I don't even owe you a tip. That is the brutal truth. You're supposed to do a great job in your work service. So I expect you to do your job. Tips are extra. Yet, we will reward bad service because of how we may appear to others. We have to get out of the habit of rewarding mediocrity.

A friend once called from jail. "Oh my God," she said. "I was driving ... I wasn't that drunk. I mean, I was just tipsy and I got arrested for DUI. Can you please put some money on my books?" You know what my response was? "Hell no! I can't put spending money in your prison account. I'm not rewarding bad behavior. Period. You know the law and you put everyone on that road in danger for a couple of swigs. Call somebody else."

Every time someone asks you for something, remember that their decision-making got them where they are, good or bad. You don't have to allow your time, money, or influence to be used to help them out of a bad situation they put themselves in, nor should you feel bad about it.

Saying no should make you feel great. It is a boundary—a *healthy* boundary. It's one step toward self-empowerment and another way to say, "You are not going to take advantage of me." You don't owe anyone anything—and that includes explanations.

Boundaries Are Power

You have a voice, and your voice matters. Not only that, but your voice is the ONLY one that matters in your life. When you know your voice matters, it is very easy to set boundaries.

Don't allow people to put you in a situation where you're intimidated to talk or ask a question. One where you're too scared they'll laugh at you or judge you in some way. Screw that. Never be afraid to ask a question. I tell students that all the time. It is not good to sit there confused, especially in a place like a classroom. Who cares if the people next to you, your classmates, think it's a stupid question. I promise you, they're just as confused as you are, but they're too scared to ask. The only difference between you and the student next to you is that you opened your mouth and asked a question.

The same is true outside of a classroom setting. When you are able to ask questions, to be bold, and move without fear, you show that you're not scared. You show that you have a voice and that your voice matters. And you show your boundaries—that you will not allow someone else's voice or outside influence to overpower your own.

This has happened to me many times on set, with directors or stunt coordinators unable to articulate or convey what they want. Well, I'm doing stunts and safety is my priority, so I'll be damned if I'm about to perform a stunt if there is any confusion about what we're attempting. I want to get home to my family at night the same way all the other cast and crew want to get home to their families: safe.

If anything is unclear to me, I will ask: "What are we doing here? What do you want me to do? Are we doing 'three, two, one, action'?" All my questions are to ensure clarity on what is being asked for the stunt. When I have that clarity, there is a confidence and assurance for proper execution and safety. I don't care if their eyes are rolling while I'm asking my questions. Their eyes mean nothing. At the end of the day, my safety and the safety of my cast and crew is what matters.

You create boundaries by knowing you have a voice and, as such, power. My voice matters, and I don't care what you think, because I have a voice. If you have a problem with me using my voice, that means you were trying to have power over me.

Even when it's something simple, like the food you eat at an establishment. We could take a poll right now about how many people have eaten an order that a restaurant got wrong. There'd be so many people out there saying, "Yeah, I just said, 'OK, whatever,' and ate it, even though I didn't want to." Why would you do something you don't want to do? Why, when that waiter brought you the wrong food, did you not give it back? Did you not articulate your order clearly? Did you not tell them you have an allergy? Why would you eat something that you don't like?

You have a voice. It means something. Use it.

Taking Back Your Power

You may have surrendered your power in the past, but that doesn't mean you can't reclaim it. It simply takes action—make the pivot to being someone who says no and sets boundaries. That's all it takes. It's not rocket science.

You don't have to announce to anyone that this change is underway, that a change in power is on the horizon. But if you want to, have a conversation with those who have been treating you in a way that you won't permit moving forward. That might look a little something like this:

"Hey, I need to talk to you. I've been noticing some stuff, and it doesn't work for me. Please don't talk to me that way. Please don't handle me that way. Please don't deal with me that way."

But again, you have no obligation to put people on notice. In fact, in some situations, it might be better not to. Just make the change and move forward. Regardless, reclaiming your power means taking action. When I ran track and got second or third place in a meet, I didn't tell everyone that I was going to work harder, practice more, and improve—I simply did it. Take your responsibility and your power back by doing, by changing, and by embracing your voice. Use it. You are the sole decision-maker of your life.

Accepting Your Power

You have the ability to move, disengage, and become the person you're destined to be. You have the power to be the person you want to be and do the things you want to do. All it takes is making sure you don't let anyone deter you from your dreams, your aspirations, and your goals.

Life isn't easy, but there are some things you can do that *are* easy. Making good decisions is not hard. You know smoking is bad for your heart and your lungs, but you're telling me it's hard to stop? If I go to a doctor and he tells me I'm on the verge of a heart attack, it seems like quitting would be a very easy decision to make if I want to live, right? So, what are we talking about here?

I think we are making life very complicated by refusing our power and instead are becoming comfortable with excuses and wrongdoing. People are so comfortable being in these unsavory places that they will say doing right is too hard. But it's not hard to do right—you just don't want to.

Every day, doctors and nutritionists show people how their food and drink choices are killing them. Yet people say they can't stop eating all these pizzas and drinking all these sodas. It's just not true. You are the one who bought the soda instead of water. It's not like you went into an actual soda mart. You went to a grocery store with options: fruit and protein and salad and ice cream and frozen pizza. You had options, and you chose the wrong ones for your health, and now you are telling the doctor it's hard for you to stop eating. Shame on you. Shame ... on ... you. That's your accountability and your responsibility.

Life is an experience, and your experience will be based on your decisions. Be smart in your decision-making while understanding that even with good decision-making, difficult, unexpected stuff will still happen. That's life. We're not prognosticators, but everything is not going to go according to plan.

I have vision boards. There are things I will accomplish. It's not for me to know when or how. However, I walk as if they're going to happen because they're on my vision board. My decision-making through the process will be smart, so I'll put myself on a clear path toward these desires.

I don't buy into the easy-hard thing because it's decision-making. In the same way you made the wrong decision, you can make the right one.

If your thoughts, psychological makeup, and emotions were a team, your mindset would be the coach. You want to create a coach that tells you, "Go out and win. You've got this!" I don't think anybody would play for a coach who'd say, "Hey, you're going to lose today. I'm just letting you all know." Saying that this type of coach would not have a good record would be an understatement.

Your mind is the coach, but you are the MVP, the player who has the power and the decision-making prowess to go with whatever the coach says. For this formidable team to be successful, however, you must have both on the same page. Any team filled with the best players who are playing a different game from their coach is not going to make it to the championship. That's like having a director and starring actor working on the same movie, but shooting different scripts.

It's not enough to have your coach, i.e. mindset, on the right track if the player isn't going to repeat the coach's message—and vice versa.

If you're saying, "I have the power," but your inner coach is saying, "I don't know about today, man. I don't think I can. It's not going to work," you are not in alignment. Remember, this is your circus and your monkeys. You are the ringmaster of your own life. You are the lion, you are the dogs jumping through the ring of fire, you are the elephant with the girl on the top throwing you the peanuts, you are the juggler, and you have to keep all these aspects aligned. If you don't, it throws everything off. It messes up the whole thing, and you'll have to start over.

Rule #6:
Have Faith

Having grown up going to church my whole life, God was instilled in me in the womb. I grew up with knowledge of God, Jesus, and faith. In church, you're taught that faith is the substance of things hoped for and the evidence of things unseen. As you get older, you can take that definition and spirit of faith and apply it to other areas of your life.

Why Faith Matters

Faith, for me, is knowing that no matter what situation I'm in and what concerns I have, everything will always work out in my favor because God has my back. I walk and navigate knowing I'm a child of the King, and when you're a child of the King, you know He has you. I have confidence, trust, and dependence on God.

Faith is connected to knowing that the creator, at the end of the day, is the ultimate decision-maker. When you have faith, you allow God to work His magic. You allow God to use the people around you and in your life as pawns to dish out the blessings, the instruction, and the correction you need, all for your good.

I've seen what faith can do. I've seen the results that come from having faith. I had faith that I was going to get *Black Panther*. I prayed every day—because faith and prayer go hand in hand. You're praying to the one who has the ultimate decisions, the person who you know can make things happen.

Not only does God make things happen, He will send people to you as confirmation, letting you know, "Hey, I'm working on this for you." When I was doing acting and stunts, there was a movie, *Captain America: Civil War*, and all the Black people were working on it—except me. I thought, "How are these Black people working on *Captain America: Civil War*, and I'm not?" At the time, I was working on TV shows, like *True Blood*, but I really wanted to work on a Marvel movie. I even had it on my vision board—so I was confused about why I wasn't working it.

One of the girls who was working on it called me and said, "I'm at *Captain America: Civil War*. They've got this guy Chadwick here, he's playing the Black Panther. They said they're giving the Black Panther his own movie. They're going to need Black women just like you who can fight, so make sure your fighting is up to date." Immediately when she told me, I said, "That's God. That's confirmation. I'm going to Marvel."

Boom. Every day after that, I prayed. "Thank you, God, in advance for *Black Panther*." I knew that He had sent that message through my friend. She was a pawn in the ultimate plan for the blessing over my life. Her call was God saying, "I got you. I heard you. You're not going to be in *Captain America: Civil War*, but I'm going to prepare you for *Black Panther*. I got you."

Aligning Yourself with God

If you have faith, that means you are giving all trust and dependence to God, and you are in alignment and believe He is going to do it. Whatever "it" is. You can't have faith and not believe that the creator is going to make it happen for you.

Faith goes hand in hand with believing that the source you give the faith to has the power to make it happen. I navigate this planet only by giving full faith to the creator. I do not give it to man, but I understand that the creator will use man as a blessing and a pawn. Only the creator has the ultimate power and the ultimate say-so. The rest of us are pawns in His game.

I've been used as a pawn many times to be a blessing for other people. So have you. We're all pawns on God's chessboard being moved around where people are checkmated all day long. There is peace of mind that is attached to knowing things are going to work out for your good.

My faith in God brings me peace. It calms me down, and I wouldn't even be able to tell you where I'd be on this planet if I didn't have faith, trust, or belief in God.

When I was in college, my mom died, and I watched people who knew her, even family members, go crazy with grief. They lost it. Of course, I was sad. I was terribly sad. That was my mom. My primary guardian was gone. But when I was in that hospital room watching her in that bed, the only thing I could say was, "Thank you, God. Thank you, God."

I was saying, "Thank you, God, that you gave me my mom, who instilled so much in me that has created this relationship with you so that I know I'm OK. I know I'm good."

If I didn't have God, I wouldn't be here. If my mom wasn't smart enough to make sure that we had that relationship, I don't know where I would be.

And that's the point—it is a relationship. There are people who go to church every day who have no relationship with God. I am so grateful I have a relationship, and because my relationship is so strong, I was able to get through the worst part of my life—when I lost my primary guardian.

Not only was it a time of mourning, it was a time of feeling blessed. I felt so incredibly blessed because my mom made sure I had a relationship with God that would always bring me peace. She gave me the tools I needed to learn more and develop a closer relationship with God. She helped me see His omnipotent power so that I would never forget what He can do.

In later years, when I was fired from a job for speaking up against people, I was OK with that because I did the right thing. My time on that job was up. I knew that it wasn't the right job for me and God had something better. This was all part of the plan. That job was a lesson. Whatever tools I gained on that job were to help me be better along the way.

I know that the place where I currently am is never how my story is going to end. There are always steps to the next level. From elementary school until now, it has all been a process of leveling up, and I will keep striving and reaching higher.

The Sacrifice Never Outweighs the Reward

Even when our dreams are coming true, accepting them may involve making sacrifices. But remember this: Your sacrifice will never outweigh your reward.

When I was offered *Black Panther,* I almost didn't take the job because I didn't want to shave my head. I thought I was going to look like a boy, and in retrospect, I can say that it didn't matter—but it did.

There is a strong attachment to hair in the African American culture. It's a part of our identity and how we express ourselves. My hair was twenty-six inches down my back. It was long, soft, and healthy. Even though I had Marvel Studios on my vision board and had prayed six months straight for my role in *Black Panther*, that did not matter. The mere fact that the role required me to shave my head was enough for me to second-guess what I had been consistently praying for. Hair attachment is real!

I cried long and hard, for days, at the thought of being bald. I talked to my brother John and shared my concerns with him. He said, "You're not going to look like a boy. If you're cute, you're cute! And your hair grows back." I talked to a friend who said, "Why are you crying over hair? Are we really crying over this? Didn't we just pray about this?"

Then I talked to my pastor at my church, Pastor Hosea Collins, and explained to him the dilemma I was going through. He said, "Haven't we prayed for this? You had the entire church praying for you. Jesus sacrificed it all on the cross, and you mean to tell me you can't sacrifice your hair? I'll tell you this: Your sacrifice will never outweigh your reward."

Talk about a gut punch and reality check all rolled into one! After that conversation, I accepted the job and eventually had my head shaved. And it would continue to get shaved every morning while shooting the film. But here is the kicker. Here is the blessing. Nine weeks into shooting the film, I received an email while on set that stated I was going to be needed for another Marvel Studios project!

What I almost turned down became my invitation into the Marvel Cinematic Universe. I literally became a superhero! I received ample work because of that initial head shave. That initial sacrifice. My obedience in following through with the blessing God gave me by shaving my head, which was my sacrifice, rewarded me greatly.

Your sacrifice will never outweigh your reward. Always remember that.

Once I worked on a popular horror film and the lead actress was very nasty and disrespectful to me. I told her, "You can't talk to me like that. You're going to have to lower your voice modulation." She didn't like that. She would rather speak disrespectfully toward me. So she went and lied to the producers and I ultimately got fired with two days of work remaining. Within that same week, I was offered another job that gave me a more prominent role. When you have the faith, you know that in every situation, especially the situations where you've done good and have to stand on that mountain by yourself, God has got you, and your reward will be great.

A full head of long, healthy hair! This was taken on August 13, 2016, less than three months before Janeshia booked the role of a Dora Milaje in the Marvel Studios action film, Black Panther, *for which she had to shave her head.*

During her head shave, Janeshia had the Marvel barbers put her hair in ten braided ponytails and then clip them so she could save her hair and use it as part of her testimony for speaking engagements.

Accelerating Your Faith

If you're struggling with your faith, remember that belief and faith go hand in hand. If you have faith that someone has the answers to make a situation work out, then you have to believe that it's going to work out. That's faith. Faith allows you to train your mind to believe you will be victorious. Faith is what lets you know the end result before you can see it. And the end result is always victory.

As such, your faith has to be in alignment with your belief system. You have to let God do His thing while He sees that you have faith in Him to do it. Get your mindset right and know that not only is everything going to work out, but it will work out in your favor.

Finally, don't get caught up in religion. Instead, remember it's about your relationship with God. If you focus on the religion, then you're going to get caught up somewhere and not like the pastor or the people you're sitting next to in the pews. When this happens, you're focusing on the messenger, not the message.

Where is your relationship with the creator? The one you can go to any time of day? The one whose phone is never busy? With that relationship, you can be vulnerable and honest when you talk to Him. I know I talk to him; I scream and yell sometimes too.

Ultimately, you have to understand that you are worthy of it working out. You deserve a win, but you're not going to get that win on your own. Some wins have to come through faith. You're going to have to have the faith sometimes to know this, "OK, all right, God, universe, make it work. I'm trusting you, universe. I'm giving full trust to you. You've got this. Put the people in my life to make this happen, God. Whatever it is."

Braving the Loneliness of Faith

When you have faith, there will be times when the only person rooting for you is you. Sometimes, you will be in enemy territory—and that's when your faith needs to be strongest.

God said He would prepare a table before me in the presence of my enemies. And God does not lie. So, I have faith knowing that amid my enemies, I will prevail. God serves me plates of blessings that include prosperity and abundance, and I eat very well. My enemies see His good works. They see His light shine through me because I'm navigating this planet only to please Him. I'm edifying Him, putting my faith and trust in Him because He is the decision-maker. God has the power. Everyone else is a pawn He uses to bless and carry out His plans.

When you find yourself in enemy territory, I want you to remember something my mom always said: "God will never put on you more than you can bear." I know everything I get, I can handle, but I also don't have to handle it alone because God is right there with me.

Sometimes, your turf becomes enemy territory when you invite the wrong people in. Keep your home turf in alignment with your faith. Never invite in people who are contradictory to what you believe, because then you're doing yourself a disservice. It's like having a bad player on your team. Or a spoiled piece of fruit in the bunch. It will be challenging for you to have faith and accomplish your missions when the people around you are saying, "That's not going to work out. Why do you want to do that? That's too hard."

Instead, keep people around you who believe you deserve to win. People who have a dialogue without negativity and limitations. During the pandemic, I was working. A lot. I counted every COVID test I took.

I posted and documented everything. Many people said, "Oh my God, everybody's getting COVID."

I said, "Hold up. Who's everybody?"

Their response was always, "You haven't gotten it yet?"

In response, I would say, "*Yet*? What's wrong with your thinking? COVID *yet*? Who says I have to get it? I'm not going to get COVID. Me and God had a conversation. I'm not going to get it. How about that? The nerve of you to ask, 'Did I get COVID yet?' Shame on you."

You have to be able to shut people down when they say something stupid in your presence or when they speak things over your life and make you a part of the masses. Not everyone in the Bible was affected by a plague. Everybody on the planet did not and will not get COVID. But the nerve of someone to even use dialogue like that in my presence—I immediately shut it down.

Faith doesn't cost a thing. It's simply about understanding that someone greater than you has all the answers to your issues and questions, and that your faith, when aligned with your belief, will give you results that work out in your favor.

Rule #7:
Play Fair: Morals

I've defined morals to be the standards that you set for your behavior. They help you decide what actions are right and which ones are wrong. They guide you to see what's ethical and what isn't, and dictate your overall behavior.

Society is very big on people getting to the top by any means necessary. Where does that leave morals such as honesty and fairness? It means they go right out the window. Our society is supportive of those who lie about people to steal their position. How far behind is shooting or stabbing to get what you want?

My morals dictate the standard for how I behave, what's right and what's wrong, and what's honest. My mom always said, "You don't have to stab anybody in the back to get where you need to go." So, in my everyday life, I have to think, "Is that right? Does that help me? Does that help someone else? Am I lying? Am I being deceitful?"

I have gotten where I am today by being truthful, honest, dependable, and reliable, and not sacrificing the morals I was raised on.

What It Means to Live Your Morals

If you're using your morals the right way, then when someone asks you about someone you don't like, you will be honest. For instance, I didn't like Kobe Bryant. He wasn't my favorite player, but if you asked me about Kobe, I'd say, "That dude was a great player. He worked hard and had a great work ethic." I would be lying through my teeth if I didn't give that man his credit. I don't have to like you to be honest about you, because my morals tell me to be truthful, honest, and fair. I don't need to lie and say you did something that you didn't do to make you look bad.

Instead, I can be honest about what you bring to the table, your skills, and how you treat people. You don't have to like someone to be honest or fair when speaking about them.

If your moral compass isn't enough to keep you choosing the honest and truthful way, remember this: When you have good morals and you operate in a moral fashion, you have fewer bad consequences. I don't want bad consequences, so by default, I operate at a high level of what is morally right, fair, and honest. When a person operates that way, they will sleep well at night. The universe returns good.

The Bible says, "You shall reap what you sow." There is no way that I would be writing this book and doing all these commercials and movies if I were not a good, moral person. It just wouldn't work. People wouldn't even talk to me. They wouldn't come to see me at comic cons. I wouldn't be as blessed as I am.

All these actions—or, as I've mentioned throughout this book, *decisions*, are the results of each other. Everything goes hand in hand. Morals, accountability, faith, trust.

Do you remember WWJD? What would Jesus do? It may sound cliché, but that's the simple principle that guides my life. I haven't perfected it—I'm still working on forgiveness, for example. But even though I'm not perfect, just understanding that I am in this aligned relationship with God compels me to operate and navigate a certain way. I have to have good morals, I have to be honest, and I have to be able to stand by myself and speak out when I know something is wrong because it's morally right.

One of the greatest examples I've seen of someone acting in a faithful, moral way occurred during the Columbine shooting. One of the victims, a young girl, was in a classroom when one of the shooters came in and asked her if she believed in God.

Witnesses say that she answered the shooter in the affirmative—that she did believe in God. You know why she said that? Because her faith, trust, and dependence on God were bigger than anything that was going on. She didn't answer based on what she thought the shooter wanted to hear or whatever might save her life. She answered her truth. And what she was really saying was that she knew she would be all right, regardless of what the outcome was. She knew that God had her back, and that's the same way I was raised. I trust and depend on Him.

That girl had more balls than anybody I know. To have her faith tested in the presence of enemies—with a gun held to her—and she did not back down. She didn't cower and she didn't weaken. She didn't mull it over, none of that. She was very secure in her reply.

I, too, am this secure with my faith and my morals. As such, I'm not going to stab anybody in the back, and I'm not going to neglect my God. I will not throw everything my mama instilled in me out the window. I will be truthful, I will be honest, and I will navigate life by those standards.

Faith helps in this, because having faith means I know I don't have to stab anybody in the back to get where I need to go. I can help people along the way without feeling threatened, insecure, or that they're coming for my job, because I have the faith, trust, belief, and dependence that God will get me where I need and want to go.

The Freedom of Truth

Earlier in the book, I told you that God was instilled in me while I was still in the womb. Also instilled in my prenatal psyche were my mom's morals. From early in life, the lessons she taught us included, "You have to be honest, even in the face of adversity. Even when there are 20,000 people on the other side of you who are lying, you'd better stand up and be truthful." When I look around society today, I think that we have lost our honesty factor. People think that it's OK to be partially truthful, but let me tell you something: part lie and some truth is still lie. Period. You can't mix it. You're either being truthful or you're lying.

I've learned both from my mother and my own life experiences that there is freedom that comes with being completely truthful. You don't have to remember what you said or walk on eggshells or live with a fear of being exposed. Essentially, there's no bondage in truth-telling.

Truth-telling has become such a rare trait today that modern society has a whole new name for it: whistleblowing. I will never take on that title as a whistleblower. I'm a truth-teller. When are we going to start giving titles to the liars? When will we assign titles to the dishonest, the mischievous, and the unsavory?

Never be afraid to tell the truth or to stand up for yourself. When you start standing up for yourself, you're going to attract a different type of person, because the people you have to stand up against aren't going to want to stick around. They don't want to deal with you anymore because they see they have no power over you. You're too honest with yourself now. You have taken back your power. You are aware that you have control.

They say the truth can set you free, and I agree that being truthful is freedom. I also believe that people who lie to themselves are in bondage. Lying is a trap that doesn't want to let go.

My mom was my greatest teacher. I've already talked about how she gave life lessons to my twin sister and me, preparing us to be high-functioning individuals. That's how we became so well-rounded—fluent in sign language, able to play a musical instrument, successful in oratorical contests and public speaking, competing in math-a-thons and athletics. She made sure we had all these tools because she knew we would be young Black females navigating in a world where, historically, the road to our success would be more difficult. She made sure we knew our history and where we came from and that we understood the systemic racism in place.

Doing all this, she allowed us the chance to succeed and be free, but also to be free from the bondage of lying. In the late 1990s during the Menendez brothers' trial, we asked our mom what the trial was about, and she said, "They're on trial because they killed their parents."

I said, "They killed their parents?" It was just incredible and unthinkable to me that such a thing could happen. Because my sister and I thought, "You're not supposed to do that!" And what made it even worse was, although the brothers might have had other issues with their parents, the reason for the killing was simple greed.

Now, during this time, my mom brought home a manila envelope with a bunch of money in it. She asked us to count it, then she went back outside, got in her car, and left.

A short time later she returned and asked us if we counted the money. We told her we had and when she asked how much it was, we told her. She said, "Very good. That was the best thing you could've done. You not only counted the money, but you were honest about how much it was. You think I didn't know how much money it was? I knew exactly how much money it was. I wanted to know if you girls were going to be honest or try to take some of the money."

It sounds like such a simple lesson, but she took it further. She said, "Don't ever be so focused and driven by money that you will lie for it or steal from your parents. Those two Menendez boys were so caught up in this that they killed their parents out of greed."

She then said, "It's not money that's bad. Did that money do anything to you guys? Did it hit you? Did it slap you? Did it cuss you out? Did it do anything?"

"No. We just counted it."

"Exactly," she said. "It's never the money. It's the love and the greed for the money. The money their parents had didn't hurt those Menendez boys. That was their greed, their desire. Don't you ever be so caught up and tied up to where you are greedy for money that you start doing things that I did not teach you to do, like cheating, stealing, and killing. You don't have to chase money. When you're operating in your purpose and your passion, you will be taken care of."

My mom was exactly right. I've navigated my career as a witness to those early childhood lessons. People are going to come to you because you're offering a skill or a product they want. You'll never have to chase money, kill anybody for money, cheat anybody out of money, or steal it—and if you want it that bad, then you go work for it. You don't take someone else's.

Morals Are Not Limitations

You may have noticed that when my mom was teaching my sister and me about being moral, honest people, she did not treat these traits as though they were a limitation. She did not say we could not earn as much if we were honest; she said we wouldn't even need to chase money.

Just as being truthful gives you freedom, being moral gives you access to limitless success. In our home, there were a lot of expectations. We were expected to always do our best and give 100 percent; we were expected to be accountable and disciplined; and we were expected to have dreams.

As such, vision boards were a big part of my childhood. My mom didn't speak to us in limitations. We could not say the words "hard" or "can't" in our household. Those two words just did not exist. "You can do all things through Christ who strengthens you," Philippians 4:13.

I operate out of abundance. That's why I can help you *and* help myself. I don't feel like you're going to take from me. There's plenty for everybody.

When you look at the details, not everyone has the same set of morals, but there are some nonnegotiables on what's right and what's wrong. Doing right is not rocket science. Stop making doing what's right a challenge. It's not. Adjust your moral compass to where doing what's right and what's fair and what's honest is at the top and not at the bottom.

You do not get to turn your morals on and off. They have to always be on. Accountability, always on. Truthfulness, always on. Your power and decision-making has to always be on. Your grind and your hustle, always on. Everything is on. These are not switches like the lights in your house. This is energy that has to be going constantly. That way, when people come to you with things that are contradictory to your plans for your life, you can turn their switches off.

Rule #8:
Stay Patient

Because success doesn't happen overnight, we all need to work on our patience. Patience is the ability to tolerate delays without being upset, anxious, or mad.

When you're patient with yourself, you have an internal monologue that reassures you everything is going to be OK and that when obstacles pop up, you'll get through them. You could be on track to getting exactly where you need to go and then, boom, injury happens, the market crashes, you lose a job, or your house heads into foreclosure. All these different life circumstances and situations might pop up on your journey and create a slight hurdle, hiccup, or delay, but patience is what helps you not melt down during the situation.

Patience helps you stay focused on the end result or goal when the detour changes your path.

Patience Is Not a Pause

Patience may mean accepting a delay, but it is not an excuse to abandon your plan of action. While you are being patient, you're not just sitting around doing nothing. You should still be actively doing things. You can still train, work on your skills, learn something new, deepen your knowledge, and more.

When an athlete suffers an injury and can no longer play, they are encouraged to do rehabilitation and physical therapy—not to relax and do nothing. I say this all the time: The universe responds to activity, not inactivity. When a hurdle pops up in your life, you can still be moving forward.

When COVID-19 happened and Hollywood shut down, it didn't stop the fast-moving train I was on. I still had other things I was doing. I was patient for Hollywood to come back, but in the meantime, I started my own consignment business. I refurbished and fixed old bikes and chairs. Ask me if I have a welding license. No, I do not. Ask me if I'm a carpenter like Jesus. No, I am not. Yet there I was, fixing and selling old bikes and chairs during the pandemic for three years while I patiently awaited Hollywood's return. I continued to train and walk every day, supported local businesses, and more.

And let me tell you, I got slapped by some people in my community who asked, "Why are you going out?" I returned their frustration, asking them why they weren't doing their part to help these local businesses stay afloat. For them, patience during COVID was about inaction and fear. For me, it was about finding different actions.

Patience is a time when you keep a sane mind in the midst of the delay. It is not a time to abort and stop. Patience is not synonymous with complacency. Complacency means that instead of displaying a drive to be better, you would rather sit still and be OK with what's going on, a.k.a. mediocrity. Patience is saying, "I will let these things work out how they're going to work out, but I'll still be active. I'm still going to move, hustle, and grind."

Unlocking the next level requires patience, but it's not just about waiting. It's about actively grinding for another goal that also supports your initial pursuit.

You are never to quit. You are never to turn off the switch. That will happen when you're in the grave.

Patience through Faith

One of the most important traits that will enable you to find patience is faith. Faith helps you understand that although you don't see results happening while you're being patient, things will work out. Faith confirms that while in the midst of your storm, the sun will shine again. God will cover you, and you will end up victorious.

Part of the reason I can be patient is that I already know what's going to happen to me—no matter how delayed it is. I already know how the story ends—with me being victorious. I knew *Black Panther* was going to happen. My faith was unwavering. I was so in tune with God, and my faith aligned with what I knew He could do.

It's the same with anything I'm working toward. I speak my goals into the universe, and I know these things are going to happen. So, I walk and navigate as if they've already happened.

I am one of the leads in an action sci-fi film. We had the pleasure of shooting on location in Italy. I did not audition for the role, and I did not meet the writer until two days after I arrived in Italy. That's almost unheard of in my industry. It was a year ago that I said I wanted to work in Italy. I was talking to my friend who'd been there for a whole month working on a Christmas movie. He would share with me what he did and all the pictures from his hotel. "I'm going to work in Italy," I said. Not even a year later, I was working in Italy on a movie with that friend. That is the power of speaking things into existence.

I got my start acting in commercials, many of them for cars. One time, I heard about an upcoming Toyota commercial where they needed a stunt woman to do roller derby, mountain climbing, and a bunch of other activities. I was like, "Oh my God, I got this. I can do this. This is me. I've got to book this job."

I secured an audition, but it took so long to get started that I contacted the casting director directly, a friend of mine who I knew was working on it, and a few other people directly working on the commercial. They put me on avail, which, in the industry, means you are one of their favorites and are in the final stages of the casting process. It is the step right before the actual booking.

After two days of being on avail, I booked the commercial.

Generally, car commercials are shot over a week and can be multiple spots. An actor can be booked for a single spot or several of them. After booking the commercial, I went to San Francisco for the fitting of the spot I got—which was the roller derby part. While they did my fitting, someone asked if I was the woman who'd been emailing them about the mountain climbing and other spots. I said that I was, and they said that someone was reaching out to me for that spot as well.

Now, I didn't know that it was two different spots. I thought it was just one commercial. So I started emailing people to make sure I could do both parts. It turned out that I could, and also that they'd booked me on a third spot to drive the car itself.

Once I went into that first fitting and they asked if I was the one who'd been emailing them, I had been shown that God had done His work. I was in the mix. Things were being done. This is why faith is so important. I didn't have to do all that excessive emailing; it wasn't necessary. I was second-guessing my faith when the notifications took longer than I expected.

But I'm here to remind you—things are happening behind the scenes that will have situations work out in your favor. Patience can feel like loneliness. The time it took for me to get the audition notification seemed like ages! That is when my faith needed to be at its strongest. I let a little doubt creep in, which sparked all the emails and me trying to do God's work.

That situation was a good learning lesson. We have to control and be mindful of what we let in our heads. You cannot allow even the smallest sliver of doubt to occupy space in your mind. That's why I say you don't have to wait for the period, you can leave at the comma. You can't allow anything to go against what you are aligning for yourself. You can't allow negativity to be spoken over your life. When you're saying and putting things into existence, you have to believe it. The universe will align. It will dish it back to you. When you can hold on to that, patience is very easy to have.

Janeshia (in pink) in the Nike Delicious Training ad campaign.

Janeshia, better known as FROST the Olympian in WOW Women of Wrestling, doing her signature leg drop on wrestler Tatevik the Gamer. The character FROST is based off Janeshia's real-life experience as a US National Bobsledder where Frost was her nickname.

Janeshia pinning down her opponent, Tatevik the Gamer, at a WOW Women of Wrestling match in Las Vegas.

Janeshia on location in San Francisco for a Toyota commercial where she booked the role of Roller Derby Girl.

Janeshia after a successful belt test in taekwondo at Yushen Lai Taekwondo Academy.

The Test of Patience

We're put through tests to see where we are on the scale of improvement and development. We are tested in school all day. Tests see if we are ready to go to the next grade, to apply lessons we've been taught, to show that we can succeed in the next phase of our lives.

I think God does that too. God sends tests all the time. He tests our faith, our belief in His power, in His knowledge, and in the safety we have through Him. They're life lessons to develop you. Everything happening in life is to develop you at some point or another. Life is an experience, and your decision-making will determine if it is good or bad.

Some people who are in jail decided to make bad decisions, and that landed them in jail. Now, as a result of their choices, they must experience life with no freedom.

My pastor, Bishop Keith Clark, once told me, "God's delay is not a denial." You're going to get what God has planned for you, but it might not be at the time you wanted. It's going to happen, but along the way, you might have made some choices that have interfered with His plan, and now you're going to have to be extra patient to get back on track. You must get out of the driver's seat and give God back the steering wheel. Show Him that you do trust, that you do believe. You're going to get what was always planned for you, but it's going to be on God's time.

It's like when you wait too long to send your Christmas presents and you've missed the cutoff. The recipients are still going to get the presents, but not on Christmas Day. They'll probably get them on New Year's Eve or the next year.

God will always give you what He's got for you, but we can interrupt that with our decision-making, and then you have to be extra patient. Let's make it an issue to be mindful of our decision-making so that it does not interfere with God's plan. But also remembering that God's delay is not a denial.

Unsustainable Instant Gratification

It's important to understand that instant gratification does not sustain you. You have to be in this for the long game to receive the happiness and freedom that sustains.

When you're operating solely off quick, instant moments, it's not life-fulfilling, it's moment-fulfilling. You don't want that because you're going to encounter resistance at some point, like a tug-of-war, when you're doing things just for instant gratification and they're boosting your life through fake, temporary acts. You won't be able to keep up.

When your actions support the long game, when you act out of truthfulness, along the tenets of your moral compass, you have peace. Peace and patience are a powerful combination. They offer you an environment where you can talk to yourself and ask questions. You can be real. You can explore what you really want to do and what you want to accomplish. It becomes more than just trying to imitate somebody else, trying to shine through somebody else, trying to look good for somebody else. It becomes about the person in the mirror. It becomes about you.

When you discover what it is you want to do, truthfulness and authenticity will resonate. You will understand and be in alignment with the patience necessary for you to maximize and become what you want to be.

But you won't reach that level if you are focused on instant gratification, because you're not taking that half a beat to reflect and assess what you want to do. You're so busy trying to go by society's standards that you have none of your own.

Society will force you to color in the lines like everybody else. I'm telling you: color outside the lines. There's beautiful art made there. But you will not get outside the lines until you understand what you want—until you understand you have power and that you have to keep your light switch on and not give away your power.

Stop chasing what society wants you to do. Don't give in to the pressure. Stop going for instant gratification. Society is a trend. You won't be able to sustain it because it will keep changing on you. Before you can even get good at what they want you to do, something else comes out. Society is just like an iPhone. You can't keep up with it. The moment you buy one, another version comes out, in more sizes and colors.

Instead, take half a beat to assess what *you* want to accomplish and who *you* want to be. Make that art outside the lines. Color and scribble, do whatever you've got to do, and it will be more fulfilling, sustaining, and authentic than anything done for instant gratification.

When you operate in the space that you want to be in, you will understand the power you possess. Too many people don't understand the power they have because they're not coloring outside the lines. They're operating within the lines, parameters, and constraints of someone else, with all the other sheep and cattle.

Rule #9:
Breathe

Life can be overwhelming. That's a cold, hard fact. When you are overwhelmed, you can develop anxiety and other physical, emotional, and psychological ailments triggered by the pressures and the demands you feel. No matter how much pressure you feel both within and outside yourself, it's important to take a beat and breathe.

Earlier in the book, I told you about my softball coach asking me to take a beat before throwing the ball. When you take that beat and you breathe, you understand that you are alive. This helps put your life and progress into perspective and can show you how much more there is to do—and none of it will get done unless you're breathing.

It's not just on the softball field where I have to be reminded to breathe. Throughout the process of writing this book, I have been super juiced, motivated, anxious, and inspired. I'm like a fast-moving locomotive, and I still have to tell myself, "Girl, breathe. It's all going to get done, but you still need your brain. You don't want your brain to get overloaded."

I am constantly, actively pursuing whatever I'm aiming for, but in that pursuit, I've still got to breathe—and so do you. Doors will open for you because of what you're doing, and it might be a little overwhelming. The best way to deal with that is simply to breathe.

The Power of Breath

Throughout this book, I've talked about how these methods I'm sharing will help give you time and power to reflect and truly isolate what you want from life. Breathing is another one of those exercises that gives you the space and power to reflect and assess. But it's even more powerful than that because breathing can also help you overcome the chaos in your brain and accept that this, too, shall pass.

I suffer severe anxiety on planes. I get so incredibly anxious, it feels like I'm going to have a heart attack. A long time ago, I was on a flight with a pilot sitting next to me. We were going through turbulence, and I grabbed his arm out of fear. He told me it was OK and began telling me all these different things about flights, flying by wire, airlines, and the buttons in the cockpit. Then, he asked me if I got anxious like this when driving my car over a pothole. I said no, and he said, "That's exactly what this is. When you're in the plane and you feel turbulence, think in your head, *pothole*, *pothole*, *pothole*."

During his calming story, I began to breathe normally. It made me realize that my anxiety and shortness of breath were the real threat—not the plane driving over a metaphorical pothole. This stranger was able to assess the situation, ask me basic questions related to what I am used to, and redirect my thoughts enough that I was again able to breathe normally.

Breathing is so important because when you're able to calm the anxiety, your focus changes. For the duration of that flight, I was no longer focused on having a heart attack or being in a plane crash. I focused on my breathing and put the turbulence into perspective.

Like it did for me, breathing will help you shift focus if you're overestimating the power of the surrounding chaos. Life and outside forces can be chaotic, but you need to take that half beat to breathe so you can shift focus. The chaos creates confusion, but breathing will help you exit the state of confusion. It will give you peace.

Breathing Techniques

Here are a few breathing techniques that have worked for me.

Be the Timer

Count from ten to zero, like a timer.

10 ... 9 ... 8 ... 7 ... 6 ... 5 ... 4 ... 3 ... 2 ... 1 ... 0

This is your way of giving yourself time to get back to homeostasis. And don't forget the zero; the zero means it's complete.

Conscious Breathing

Conscious breathing is crucial to reflect and assess. When you have that failure or a loss, whether it be from a race or a game or you didn't get the job, take that breath and think positive affirmations to yourself. For example:

"I did my best. I performed to the best of my ability. I'm proud of myself. I gave it my all. I will be better next time. I will win next time. I will get the job the next time I apply. I will win the race next time."

Then, encourage yourself with power statements, such as:

"This is not the time to cower. This is not the time to be weak. This is not the time to give up. You are destined for greatness. You didn't get it this time, but you're going to get it next time. And now you're trained better, now you're more aware, now you're more skilled."

Remember, setbacks are part of the process, and they sharpen your tools as you go down the road toward prosperity and abundance. You're not going to win every time, but that does not mean you don't give your best every time.

Listen to Your Breathing

Your heart governs everything that's moving and flowing through your body. When that heart stops, there's no more breath or life. Use your breathing to keep your heart calm. The heart and breath work in synchronicity, like a metronome and an instrument. Take a beat to breathe, calm your chaos, and get back into that rhythm and that flow your heart wants to operate in.

Rule #10:
Make Sacrifices

Few goals can be achieved without sacrifice. In its simplest form, sacrifice means giving something up to gain a desired result.

If you know what you want to do in life, there will be sacrifices along the way. For instance, if you want to be a musician, there will be times when you have to play on a Friday, Saturday, or Sunday night. You're going to have to do events. You'll have to devote your time to rehearsals and gigs, so you might not be able to attend a friend's birthday party or go to the club or spend time with family.

Ultimately, the question you have to ask yourself is not whether you want to sacrifice, but **what** do you want to sacrifice? Are you willing to give up clubbing or bar-hopping and hanging out with your friends so you can achieve your goals? At the end of the day, if you're full throttle on what you want to be and what you want to achieve, you will make the necessary sacrifices to succeed.

Earlier in the book, I talked about how I had to shave my head for *Black Panther*. My hair was twenty-six inches down my back. I did not originally want to take on the role, because I did not want to give up my hair. As I said, hair attachment is big in African American culture. But maybe what it really came down to was that it felt like too big of a sacrifice to make. When I talked to my pastor, he made me understand. I would have to give up something to get to where I was trying to go.

I had to ask myself how badly I wanted this Marvel movie role. I'd had Marvel on my vision board. I'd been praying about landing a spot in this movie every day for six months. The opportunity and blessing had arrived, just in a different package that I would've preferred. All I had to do was sacrifice my hair to become a superhero.

So I did.

Janeshia as the stunt double for Hippolyta (played by Emmy-nominated actress Aunjanue Ellis) on HBO's Lovecraft Country. *She received an Emmy nomination for Outstanding Stunt Performance for that work.*

Janeshia as Officer Conn on the set of the ABC Studios/Shondaland drama, Station 19.

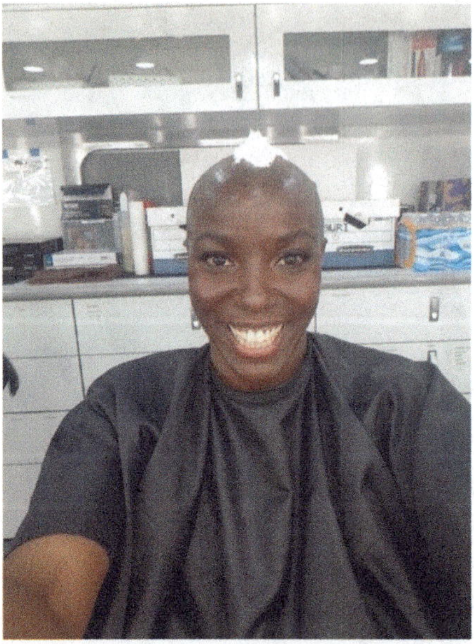

Janeshia is no stranger to having fun on and off set. Her shenanigans quite often expanded to the hair and makeup trailers.

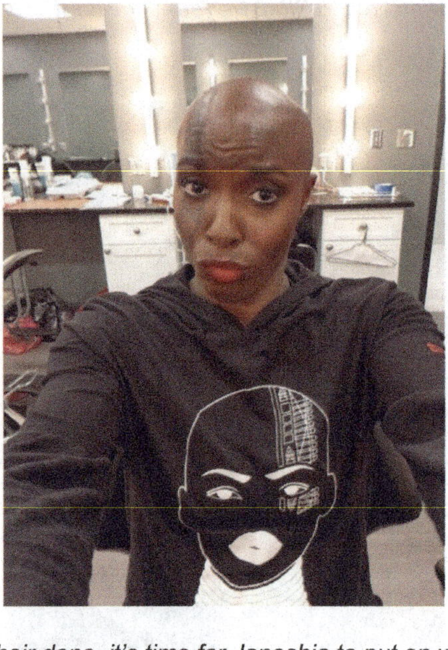

With makeup and hair done, it's time for Janeshia to put on wardrobe. On set of Black Panther.

The Test of Sacrifice

Sacrifice is required at every level of the game; it's just a matter of whether you want to play. You cannot reach the levels you're trying to achieve without sacrifice.

With almost every goal attainment process, time is sacrificed. You might be used to sleeping twelve hours a night, but when you're fully engaged in your grind and hustle, you're not going to get twelve hours. Are you willing to sacrifice four hours? Can you handle that? Can you handle the pressure?

This is another area where sacrifice is so cool. You have to see yourself at that end destination to confirm to yourself if you want to sacrifice or not. So many people don't even see themselves at the end, so it's easy for them not to sacrifice. If you don't see yourself winning and being successful, you'll have a hard time making sacrifices.

When you know that success is guaranteed, sacrifices are easier. But it takes someone who is not excuse-driven—someone who wants to put in the work—to call the shots and make the necessary sacrifices.

Sacrifices as Positives

Learning to see sacrifices as a positive thing is an essential skill for success-driven people. It's easier to do this when you understand the rules of the game. The game you're playing is life, and rules come with it. Sacrifice is one of the rules in life's rulebook.

Sacrifice is not hard. It's very simple. If you want to reach a certain level of expertise in your chosen area, you will sacrifice. You're going to sacrifice some time. You'll even sacrifice some bad relationships.

This sounds like it would be simple, but some people don't want to give up bad things. Think about someone who needs to lose weight but eats doughnuts and pizza all the time. They're clogging their arteries with bad cholesterol and choosing not to make healthier choices. They're choosing not to sacrifice their harmful relationship with food to get the physique and body they want.

So far, all of this paints sacrifice in a positive light. But one way to foster negativity in your sacrifices is to compare them to those others must make. Sacrifice is what **you** have to give up. You can't look at what you're sacrificing versus what someone else is sacrificing. Sacrifice is not one size fits all.

When I decided to pursue stunts, I researched stunt work as a career. My mom always said to be a student of the sport. As mentioned, I knew I needed to pick up some basic tumbling to know what my body would be doing in the air or while on a wire. I needed to learn air awareness and proper landing techniques to keep me and my colleagues safe. Knowing these things led me to the classes I needed to take, which helped me understand the time and money I would have to sacrifice to gain the knowledge necessary for my pursuit.

To truly understand what sacrifices might be expected of you, you need to have a detailed understanding of what your goal entails.

If you want to be a medical doctor, then you know you have years of study ahead of you, and when you reach your goal, you will be on call all the time. You will work long hours and deal with blood and trauma. Time with family and friends will become very limited, at least until your career is established.

If you research the details around your goal and realize you aren't willing to make the required sacrifices, then this goal is not suitable for you.

Staying Focused through Sacrifice

It can be frustrating when you're making sacrifices without seeing rewards or progress. Remind yourself that this is what the work is all about. You are doing this because this is what it takes to get to that level. This is nonnegotiable. You have to do it.

You are on a journey, and like all journeys, there's a payoff at the end. Try affirmations, such as saying, "This is going to pay off in the end. I'm not doing this in vain. This is not how my story ends. I do not end here. I will reach the top."

Keep your mindset strong. When you're on the journey and you're sacrificing, and you don't feel like you're seeing results, the results are in you continuing. The result is that you do not give up and instead remain on track to the end.

My mom died during my freshman year of college. I had to deal with grief and loss. I had to remind myself that my mom gave me tools early on to persevere and not give up, to know God is with me. I may have been emotionally devastated, but I knew that, at the end of the day, it was part of the circle of life. Kids are supposed to bury their parents. Parents are not supposed to bury their kids. I had to remind myself of that. I kept working and dealt with my grief, and I graduated on time.

I've sacrificed a lot of sleep to get where I am today. There have been times when I've had to do auditions while being tired as a dog. Many of these auditions have short deadlines, so you get the sides (an excerpt from a scene used for the audition) at 9:00 a.m. and have to audition at 5:00 p.m.

I've also sacrificed a lot of personal hobbies that I love, such as karaoke and bowling, because I have acting class on Monday, Tuesday, and Thursday nights. I sacrifice three hours, three times a week for acting class. If you invite me to a birthday party or a gathering or a mixer on a Monday, Wednesday, or Thursday, it's not happening. I'm not going. I have acting class, an essential tool that I need to be a better actor for my career. But it pays off each time I get a booking.

It's very easy to be lazy, and it's very easy for lazy people to make comments against those who are actively working and have nonnegotiables. Always remember, you don't have to wait for the period—you can leave at the comma. Everybody is not designed to be the winner. It's just not going to happen.

But if you desire to win, you will sacrifice what it takes, because you understand sacrifice is essential.

Rule #11:
It's Not Luck

When you find success, people will often think it's because you got lucky. Don't be afraid to tell them that, no—it's not luck. It's hard work. You are not lucky!

People see your glory, but they don't know your story. You are this amazing entrepreneur and CEO of all your companies, and they see that, but they don't see all the trials and decisions it took to get there. They don't see the moral compass that guided you, the faith that kept you going, the patience that helped you wait, the accountability you held yourself to, the gratitude you've channeled into your inner monologue, the breathing exercises that have pushed you through extreme anxiety, and the sacrifices you've made that led to your accomplishments.

Sacrifice is evident in the action. What you're doing is the result of sacrifice. I am a walking testimony to the result of a lot of sacrifices. People see the movie posters, the autograph signings, the photos. They don't know that I went to the gym three times a week before it opened, practicing my tumbling, practicing my wall flips, and then staying an additional two hours just to work on what I learned during class. That is sacrifice. The fun events I missed, the sleepless nights, the acting classes, the martial arts and athletic stage-combat training.

It took sacrifice for me to get up in the morning after my mom died. I could have stayed in bed. I could have not gone and finished the last three years of my college career and people would've been OK with it. Because I'd had a traumatic experience—losing a beloved parent—the world would have given me a major pass and an excuse to quit school.

There were times when I sat in class crying while I was doing my exams, but I had to get going. I remembered the tools my mom gave me, and I realized that giving up on college after her death would be the ultimate letdown.

That's how I shifted my mindset. Many people would've quit. But why quit? If anything, change the goal. Complete college for your mom. Go to graduation because of your mom. People have the ability to shift their goals as much as they want. They simply choose not to.

But just as my pastor said, the sacrifice has not outweighed the reward. Today I sit here talking to you as an accomplished multi-hyphenate. I am an actor and Emmy-nominated stunt performer. Did

I see myself as an Emmy nominee twelve or thirteen years ago? No. They didn't even have a category for that. I just knew I wanted to be the best stunt performer I could be.

I did the research. I was a student of the sport, and I did whatever it took to be great without sacrificing my morals.

Sacrifice pays off. I sacrificed a head of hair that ultimately landed me in a total of seven Marvel projects to date. When my head was shaved on January 4, 2017, I didn't even see the end picture. I just saw one movie. I sacrificed my hair for *Black Panther*. God said, "I have six other projects coming down the pipeline for you." Again, your sacrifice will never outweigh your reward. You are sacrificing for a small period, but your reward is so much greater, so much bigger, so much more impactful.

I hear some people right now saying, "But you were in the right place at the right time! That's luck!" No, it's not. Luck is for slot machines in Vegas. Good decision-making, grind, obedience, patience, and faith create the alignment necessary to be in the right place at the right time for God's blessings.

I would never tell someone they're lucky because I know it's not luck. Whatever they've achieved, they've done so through hard work, grind, focus, and determination. It's God answering prayers that you spoke over your life a long time ago. I have spoken things over my life and believed it, and walked as if it happened. The universe kicked back everything I said because my mindset aligned with my words, and my words aligned with my belief. My belief aligned with my faith, and all of that aligned with my decision-making.

It is nowhere near luck. This is not a pot of gold guarded by a leprechaun in a green felt hat.

Success is a journey, and it's not cutting corners. There is no shortcut to success because success is a status that is not attained overnight. It's a consistent effort to move toward a destination.

You cannot give up.

One step is better than no steps. If you want to be a writer, but you don't write anything, are you a writer? If you write one page a day, are you a writer?

You have to show progress. You can say a lot, but what are you *doing*? What do your actions reflect? You have to keep going.

The thing that separates me from people who call me lucky is that I never gave up. I am constantly moving forward. I am constantly rebranding. I rebranded myself a year ago. I rebranded myself this year. It's movement. It's work. I need to grow with the industry. When I get older, I'm going to have to play someone's grandma. I'm moving with the industry.

Success requires constant change and constant work. You've got to put in the work. A boxer is not going to train one time for one fight. They will train differently for each fighter they face. You must do the same. You must evolve.

Vibe Check

If you see where you want to be, and you see where you can go, you will sacrifice whatever it takes. The universe will come in alignment because your mindset is right. When you're being accountable to yourself and your decision-making is on, everything comes in tune.

But you are not alone on this journey. Every contact you make, every person you spend time with, is hitchhiking along for at least part of the trip—and you need to make sure they are adding value. This is what leaving at the comma is all about.

You're doing yourself a disservice if you're hanging around with people who are not speaking light, feeding into your dreams, your aspirations, and your goals. That is counterproductive to your progress and momentum.

This year, I went to Sneaker Con in Las Vegas for the first time. While I was there, I kept seeing this brand Supreme on everything. I looked it up and found out it was a skateboarding lifestyle brand. I asked someone working at the con about it, and he said the brand had done collaborations with Tiffany, Nike, Air Jordan, and more. Then he said, "There are things that you buy that are expensive and things that you buy that are valuable. Balenciaga, that's expensive, but it's not really valuable. But when you get something that has Supreme on it, you know it's valuable."

So, I ask you, are the people in your life expensive or valuable? Do they cost you stress? Do they cost you negative energy? Do they cost you dreams deferred, delayed, or denied? Or do they encourage you? Do they help you pursue what you need? If they aren't adding value to your equation, then don't wait for the period at the end of their statements. Leave at the comma.

On the set of Black Panther *during the Warrior Falls scene where the Black Panther fights M'Baku. Pictured to the right is director Ryan Coogler.*

The final day of shooting Black Panther: Wakanda Forever.

Janeshia and her horse, Milton Bradley.

Better known as the "KKK Krew," pictured from front to back: Klondike Spring Water, Krown Royal, and Kit-Kat.

Janeshia and Milton Bradley headed for a ride.

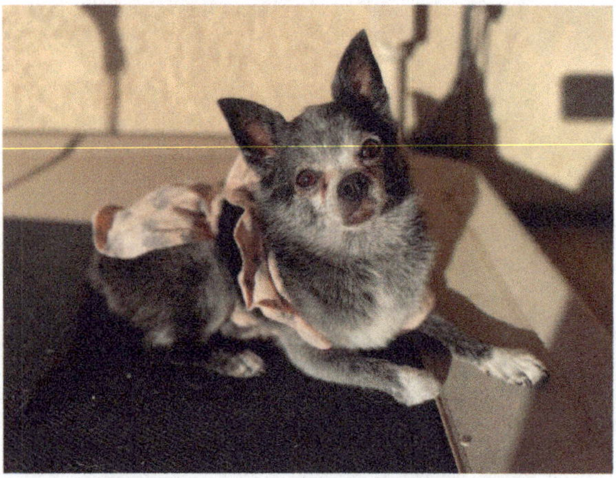

The oldest member of the "KKK Krew," Kit-Kat is fourteen. Janeshia has had her since she was one month old.

About the Author

Janeshia Adams-Ginyard is an Emmy-nominated actor, stuntwoman, wrestler, writer, and impact speaker from Southern California. Trained in taekwondo and fluent in American Sign Language, Janeshia has won three Screen Actors Guild Awards.

She has had major roles in Hollywood, including two roles in the Marvel Studios feature film *Black Panther*. In 2021, she reprised her role as Nomble, a member of the Dora Milaje, in the Marvel Studios Disney+ series, *The Falcon and The Winter Soldier*. She later starred in the films *Black Panther: Wakanda Forever* and *Letters at Christmas* and completed the action sci-fi *Lunar Lockdown* in Italy. Janeshia also did voiceover work on the 26th season of the popular animated television series, *South Park*.

Janeshia was nominated for a 2021 Primetime Emmy Award in the new category of Outstanding Stunt Performance for her work on HBO's *Lovecraft Country*.

Enthusiastic about serving God, Janeshia does ministry and helps within her community. Very active in her faith, she founded Hyphy 4 Christ, Inc., an entertainment organization dedicated to inspiring, encouraging, and motivating through faith-based content.

When not working, she spends her time traveling, doing karaoke, riding her horse Milton Bradley, and playing with her dogs Kit-Kat, Klondike Spring Water, and Krown Royal.

Made in the USA
Las Vegas, NV
17 October 2023

79268522R00066